# Terrance Talks Travel:

# A Pocket Guide to

# South Africa

South Africa

## Terrance Zepke

TERRANCE TALKS TRAVEL:
A POCKET GUIDE TO SOUTH
AFRICA

All queries should be directed to: www.safaripublishing.net

Library of Congress Cataloging-in-Publication Data

Zepke, Terrance

# TERRANCE ZEPKE

Terrance Talks Travel: A Pocket Guide to South Africa

America/Terrance Zepke p. cm.

ISBN: 978-0-9960650-1-6

1. Travel-South Africa. 2. Adventure Travel-South Africa. 3. Safari-South Africa. 4. Cape Town. 5. Kruger. 6. Africa. 7. Cape Peninsula-South Africa. 8. South Africa Guidebook. I. Title.

First edition

10 9 8 7 6 5 4 3 2 1

Safari Publishing

TERRANCE TALKS TRAVEL:
A POCKET GUIDE TO SOUTH
AFRICA

# CONTENTS

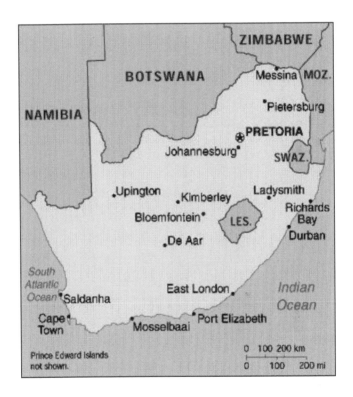

**Map of South Africa and bordering countries**

## Introduction

I love the continent of Africa. It is comprised of fifty-four countries including South Africa. I have lived and traveled all over the world, but always look forward to my visits to this extraordinary place with great anticipation. Even though I have visited Africa many times, I remain amazed by its people, topography, and wildlife. I have lived in many extraordinary places, such as London, England; Hilton Head Island, South Carolina and Oahu, Hawaii. Additionally, I have traveled to many unusual places, including the Arctic Circle, the Amazon, and Antarctica, but Africa holds a special place in my heart. It is a new and phenomenal experience every time and I think that South Africa has so much to offer, ranging from safaris to sightseeing. It offers so much that you have to know before you go that you will only be able to scratch the surface on your first visit.

There are so many things that most folks don't know about this country. It is not a developing country—far from it. In fact, South Africa has the largest economy of any African country.

It is flanked on both sides by the Indian and Atlantic Oceans. Its coastline extends more than 1,500 miles, which explains why more than 2,000 shipwrecks (dating back at least 500 years) have been found on the South African coast.

South Africa is small compared to the U.S.—about one-eighth of its size, but it is three times the size of Germany or roughly the same size as Colombia.

The oldest remains of modern humans, dating back more than 100,000 years, were found in a cave in the Eastern Cape. The Karoo region is home to some of the best fossils of early dinosaurs. Cave paintings have been discovered that date back over 75,000 years.

Furthermore, it is a wildlife lover's paradise with 200 species of mammals, 850 bird species, and more than 2,000 species of fish, as well as many species of reptiles, insects, and amphibians. Ten percent of the world's bird species can be found here, which explains why it is considered one of the best birding destinations in the world. Ten percent of the world's flowering species can be found in South Africa.

All these animals and flora and fauna can be found in the hundreds of award-winning game reserves and national parks throughout South Africa. This doesn't even include the eight UNESCO World Heritage Sites that are in this country.

Additionally, there are dozens of safari options, such as foot safaris, canoe safaris, elephant back safaris, and classic safaris. When most people think of Africa, they think of the 'Big Five' animals often seen while on safari, such

as the lion and elephant. But
South Africa also has one
hundred species of snakes,
eight species of whales, Nile
crocodiles, rare tortoises,
loggerhead and leatherback
turtles, and many species of
sharks, including the Great
White.

But South Africa has
even more to offer. They
produce some of the best wine
in the world in their charming
Cape Winelands region.

They have some of the
best island resorts in the world
on the Republic of Seychelles,
Mauritius, and Mozambique.

But there's still more.
They are known as the
"Adventure Capital of the
World." They offer too many
adventure activities to name
them all, such as kloofing,

sandboarding, bakkie skiing, rambling, canopy tours, and shark cage diving. Additionally, it is one of the best places in the world for surfing. The highest commercial bungee jump in the world (710 feet) is in South Africa.

Cape Town (and the Cape Peninsula) is a destination unto itself. It extends from Cape Point and Cape of Good Hope to Table Mountain, which is also a top tourist attraction. It has received too many awards to list, such as CNN Go's 'World's 10 Most Loved Cities' (Cape Town), Trip Advisor's Traveler's Choice 'Destination of the Year' (Cape Town), a South Africa safari was voted 'Best Family Vacation' by Family Vacation Critic and South Africa made *Conde' Nast's* coveted Gold

List. It is also a top honeymoon destination.

Due to all it has to offer, this country has recently become a major player in the movie-making industry, as well as the place many television series are filmed, such as *Homeland* and *Black Sails*. There has been so much cinematic activity here that Cape Town has been dubbed the "New Tinseltown" and "Cine City."

All of this is just the beginning. South Africa has much more to offer.

So turn the page to read, learn, and plan the ultimate adventure –a trip to spectacular South Africa!

\*　　\*　　\*

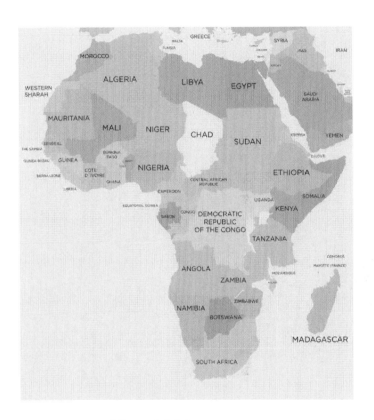

**Map of Africa**

**Fast Facts**

**SIZE:** The country of South Africa is about five times the size of Great Britain or the size of Spain and France combined (473,156 square miles).

South Africa has nine provinces:

The Eastern Cape, Free State, Gauteng, KwaZulu-Natal, Limpopo, Mpumalanga, Northern Cape, North West, and Western Cape.

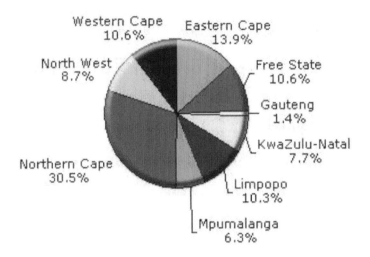

This chart shows the size of each region and the map shows the locations of all nine provinces that make up South Africa. Cape Town is part of the Western Cape while Kruger National Park is in the Gauteng province.

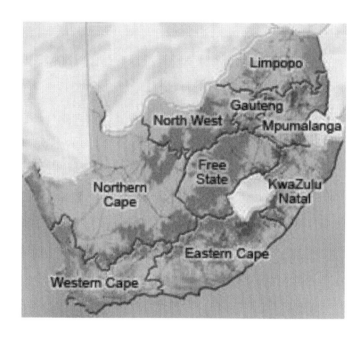

**South Africa is comprised of nine
provinces.**

**POPULATION:** Approximately fifty million. Their census classifies the people as: (79%) Black African, White (9%), Coloured (9%), Indian (2%), Asian (2%), and Other/Unspecified (0.5%).

**LANGUAGE:** South Africa has been dubbed the "Rainbow Nation" because it has such a diverse population. For this reason, there are eleven official languages: Afrikaans, English, Ndebele, Xhosa, Zulu, Northern Sotho, Sotho, Tswana, Swazi, Venda and Tsonga.

**CURRENCY:** The South African Rand (ZAR) is the currency of this country. It is issued by the South African Reserve Bank. Its name comes from the Witwatersrand ("White-waters-ridge"), the ridge where most of South Africa's gold deposits were found and where Johannesburg was built. The Rand has the symbol "R" and is subdivided into 100 cents. Coins are issued in 5c, 10c,

20c, 50c, R 1, R 2, and R 5
denominations. Banknotes include R
10, R 20, R 50, R 100, and R 200
denominations. The South African
Rand is also legal tender in Swaziland
and Lesotho, and is accepted in
Namibia. At the time of printing, the
U.S. $1 = 10 South African Rand and
1 Euro = 14 South African Rand. For
more on currency conversion, go to
www.oanda.com

**TO GET THERE:** Most
international flights arrive at OR
Tambo International Airport in
Johannesburg, but there are some
overseas flights into Durban and Cape
Town. The national airline is South
African Airways but there are dozens
of other airlines that fly into South
Africa. There are as many routes as
there are airlines, but if coming from
the U.S. I recommend flying direct
from Atlanta, GA to Johannesburg or

Washington, DC to Johannesburg. It is a long flight (18 hours) but there are no layovers or plane changes. You can fly from New York City to Johannesburg in about the same amount of time. You can also fly into Cape Town or Durban but you will change planes in Johannesburg. It is a two-hour flight from there onto Cape Town or Durban.

If flying from Great Britain, I recommend a direct flight from London to Johannesburg, which takes less than eleven hours. You can also fly from Ireland or Scotland to Cape Town in less than twelve hours. Most flights stopover in Dakar, Senegal on route to J'burg. Some visitors opt to spend a couple of days here to enjoy the West African coast. It is a popular cruise ship port of call, but be aware that tourists wishing to spend time in Dakar must have a travel visa before arrival.

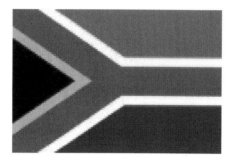

**National flag of South Africa**

**BEST TIME TO VISIT:** That depends on where you're going. The weather is quite different from one region to another. It can be sunny and hot to the north and rainy and cold to the south. Travelers should be prepared for any weather. South Africa seasons are the exact opposite of those in the U.S. When it is summer here, it is winter there and when it is winter here, it is summer there. The summer season is quite hot and popular tourist spots are very crowded, just like anywhere else. If you are planning to go on safari, the end of fall and beginning of winter is the best time. It is dry except for the occasional shower. The temps are mild and comfortable during the day. Since it is not as crowded and there is not as much greenery, you will see more animals and have a more rewarding experience.

## SOUTH AFRICA AVERAGE TEMPERATURES

In the summer months the average high is 28°C (83°F) with the average low being 8°C (46°F) Winter temperatures range from 1°C (34°F) at night to around 18°C (64°F) in the day. Note these are *averages*.

Winters are relatively mild and short. Average annual rainfall is on the low side at under 500mm (20 inches) a year, making the country somewhat dry. Much of the rain falls in the Western Cape in the winter, differing from the rest of the country, which experiences summer rainfall.

South Africa has an average of 8.5 hours of sunshine a day. Check out www.weather.com to find up-to-date weather information for anywhere in South Africa.

*FYI: It is estimated that Cape Town is 2,347 miles from the Equator.*

*Warning:*

*The temps drop quickly after sunset and early mornings are chilly, so dress accordingly. This is to be expected since South Africa is halfway between the Equator and the Antarctic. On average, ninety percent of annual rainfall occurs from November – April. However, the weather at the Western Cape (which includes Cape Town) is unpredictable year round. The last time I was in South Africa, it rained for seven days straight prior to my arrival but was dry and sunny the entire time I was there*

Seasons of South Africa...

SPRING: September, October, November

SUMMER: December, January, February

FALL: March, April, May

WINTER: June, July, August

**BUDGET:** This depends on what you're doing. International airfare will cost from $800 - $2,000 from the U.S., roundtrip, per person (on *average* for economy/coach). However, I have seen it lower and higher than this range. There is every kind of package available, from budget to luxury—or travelers can put together an independent itinerary and take advantage of special airfare and accommodation deals. Furthermore, the cost depends on how many of the components discussed in this reference you choose to include.

**UNIQUE EXPERIENCES**: There are lots of those, such as spiritual retreats, surfing camps, camel treks, horseback and elephant back safaris, hot-air balloon safaris, bungee jumping, ostrich racing, KwaZulu-Natal's Battlefields Tour, Family Adventure Safaris, and Mystery Ghost Bus Tours, which is South Africa's only national ghost bus tour. For more info, www.mysteryghostbus.co.za/

***Five things South Africa is famous for:***

***\*Surfing***
***\*Wine***
***\* Wildlife and Nature***
***\*Adventure***
***\*Culture***

**Springbok (a type of antelope) is the National Animal of South Africa.**

\* \* \*

## More Fun Facts...

Table Mountain (Cape Town) is believed to be one of the **oldest** mountains in the world and is home to more than 1,500 species of plants.

South Africa has the **longest** wine route in the world. South African wine is the **only** kind served in Disney's Animal Kingdom Lodge. South Africa has the **oldest** wine industry outside of Europe and the Mediterranean.

Kruger National Park supports the **greatest** variety of wildlife species on the African continent. Even though it is a whopping 7,500 square miles, it won't be as big as a new park in the works. South Africa, Zimbabwe, and Mozambique are teaming up to create a 13,000-square mile game reserve, which will be the **largest** in the world.

The Palace of the Lost City is the **biggest** theme resort hotel in the world as well as the largest building project undertaken in the southern hemisphere.

Tugela Falls, in the Drakensberg Mountains, is the second **highest** waterfall in the world, a close second to Angel Falls in Venezuela.

The **largest** diamond discovery was the Cullinan Diamond, which was found in South Africa in 1905. It weighed 3,106.75 carats uncut. It was cut into the Great Star of Africa (530.2 carats); the Lesser Star of Africa (317.40 carats) and 104 other diamonds of nearly flawless color and clarity. They now are part of the British crown jewel collection.

 Three of the five **fastest** land animals live in South

Africa: the cheetah, the wildebeest, and the lion.

South Africa has the **most** capitals in the world: Pretoria is the executive capital, Cape Town is the legislative capital, and Bloemfontein is its judicial capital.

*King Protea is the national plant of South Africa*

\*   \*   \*

## South Africa Historical Timeline

1400s: Zulu and Xhosa tribes establish large kingdoms in the South Africa region.

1652: The Dutch establish the port of Cape Town. They are the first Europeans to settle in South Africa.

1852: The British take control of Cape Town.

1886: Gold is discovered in Johannesburg, making the city rich.

1899-1902: Dutch settlers fight the British in the Boer War. Britain eventually gains control of South Africa.

1910: South Africa becomes an independent nation.

1918: Rolihlahla Dalibhunga Mandela is born on July 18 in a small village in South Africa. A teacher later gives him the English name Nelson.

1948: Apartheid is introduced. Laws were passed to legally and physically separate different racial groups.

1952: The African National Congress (a black civil rights group) leads a Campaign for Defiance of Unjust Laws to protest against apartheid. Nelson Mandela is one of its leaders.

1960: In the town of Sharpeville, 67 Africans are killed while protesting Apartheid.

1962: Mandela is arrested for plotting against the government. Though he stays active politically, he will spend 27 years in prison.

1966: South African government declares District Six a "whites only" area.

1982: The government sends bulldozers into District Six to destroy all buildings, except churches. More than 60,000 people were displaced when their homes were razed.

**District Six**

1990: President F.W. de Klerk announces the end of apartheid. Mandela is freed from prison after being incarcerated for 27 years.

*FYI: Robben Island prison, where Mandela spent part of his prison term, has been closed for years. However, it is open for educational tours. Interestingly, many of the Robben Island guides are former political prisoners.*

1993: De Klerk and Mandela are jointly awarded the Nobel Peace Prize.

1994: South Africa holds its first elections in which all races can vote. Nelson Mandela is elected President.

1995: South Africa wins the World Cup rugby tournament.

1999: Mandela steps down as President.

2004: The African National Congress wins a landslide election. Thabo Mbeki begins his second term as president.

2009: Jacob Zuma is elected President.

2010: South Africa hosts the World Cup soccer tournament.

Nelson Mandela, 2008

2013: Nelson Mandela is laid to rest in Mandela Graveyard at Qunu, Eastern Cape. He was 95 years old.

2015: The Public Investment Corporation, a South African government-owned financial services provider, plans to invest R2.5 billion in Africa. This will make the continent the second fastest growing region in the world after Asia.

\*　　\*　　\*

## About South Africa

To the west of South Africa is the Atlantic Ocean and the Indian Ocean is on the East Coast. The two oceans meet at Cape Agulhas, which is the only thing south of South Africa. To the north lies Namibia, Botswana, Zimbabwe, Swaziland, and Mozambique. The country is divided into nine South African Provinces. Not all of these areas are of interest to tourists. Some are uninhabited, some have nothing of interest for tourists, and some is farmland.

For this reason, this guidebook discusses these nine provinces as six significant tourism areas.

**Cape Town** is part of the Western Cape region, but it merits a separate discussion as it is the heart of South Africa and a destination in and of itself. There is much to see and do, which is why it's a favorite tourist destination. In fact, Cape Town is consistently voted a favorite place among travelers and the media, such as *Travel and Leisure*, Trip Advisor, CNN, and *The New York Times*.

Cape Town is the second most-populated city in South Africa. It is also one of the three capital cities of this country; the legislative capital. Additionally, it is the seat of the National Parliament.

It was inhabited by ancestors of Kalahari Bushmen for thousands of years before being discovered by the Europeans in 1652.

A trading post was established here by the Dutch East Indies Company. It also became home to French Huguenots, who sought asylum here from religious persecution. Later, it came under British rule. All these different influences can be seen in the architecture throughout Cape Town.

Cape Town lies on a small peninsula at the southern tip of the country. Devil's Peak is to its east while Lion's Head is to the west. Lion's Head is a mountain range that separates Camps Bay from Sea Point. It has dozens of

attractions and more than seventy
eateries, ranging from fast food to
five-star dining and includes every
kind of cuisine you can think of,
from Cape Malay to Indian.
Additionally, there are hundreds of
shops of every kind conceivable in
the greater Cape Town area.

Cape Town is comprised of
eight areas:

1. **Atlantic Seaboard** has been
   dubbed Cape Town's
   "Riviera." It stretches from the
   V & A Waterfront to the west
   side of Cape Peninsula, ending
   just before Hout Bay. It
   includes Green Point, Sea
   Point, Fresnaye, Bantry Bay,
   Camps Bay, Oudekraal, and
   Llandudno.
2. **City Centre** is commonly
   known as the City Bowl, as it is
   in a basin and the heart of the

city and includes Foreshore, CBD, Bo-Kaap, Gardens, Higgovale, Tamboerskloof, Oranjezicht, Vredehoek, and Devil's Peak.

3. **Peninsula** is where Chapman's Peak Drive is found, as well as Hout Bay, Chapman's Peak Drive, Noordhoek, Kommetjie, Scarborough, Cape Point, Simon's Town, Fish Hoek, Kalk Bay, St James, and Muizenburg.

4. **Southern Suburbs** start at the base of Table Mountain and extend all the way to Cape Point. SS includes Woodstock, Salt River, Observatory, Mowbray, Rosebank, Rondebosch, Newlands, Claremont, Kenilworth, Wynberg, Bishopscourt, Constantia and Tokai.

5. **Cape Flats** is a main residential area made up of Athlone, Crossroads, Grassy

Park, Gugulethu, Khayelitsha, Langa, Lansdowne, Manenberg, Mitchell's Plain, Nyanga and Philippi.

6. **Blaauwberg Coast** is in the Western Cape and probably the fastest-growing area, which includes Paarden Island, Milnerton, Woodbridge Island, Sunset Beach, West Beach, Table View, Bloubergstrand, and Melkbosstrand.

7. **Northern Suburbs** is another residential area. It is comprised of Century City, Goodwood, Parow, Bellville, Welgemoed, Plattekloof, Tyger Valley, Durbanville, and Bellville.

8. **Helderberg** is a beautiful area full of coastline, vineyards, and the Helderberg Mountains. It consists of Gordon's Bay, Somerset West, Strand, Sir

Lowry's Pass, Macassar, and
Lwandle.

*FYI: Cape Town is South Africa's
oldest city, which is why it is often
referred to as the "Mother City."
The first Council meeting was held
on a sailing ship in the middle of
Cape Town's Table Bay on April 8,
1652. Today, it is the second most
populated city in South Africa
(3,740,026), just behind
Johannesburg's population of
4,434,827. Not only is it the
legislative capital of South Africa,
but it is the administrative and
economic center of the Western Cape
Province.*

*FYI: A cannon is fired every day at noon from Signal Hill. The Grand Parade occurs on Wednesday and Saturday mornings. Vendors sell flowers, fabrics, toys, clothing, spices, and more. Crime is low in Cape Town but pickpockets can be a problem during these times.*

\* \* \*

## Highlights:

Table Mountain, Kirstenbosch National Botanical Garden, Greenmarket Square, Long Street, Izibo Slave Lodge, St. George's Mall, Adderley Street, Groote Kerk, South African Jewish Museum, South African Museum and Planetarium, South African National Gallery, District Six Museum, Castle of Good Hope, St. George's Cathedral, Houses of Parliament, Two Oceans Aquarium, Afternoon Tea at Cape Grace Hotel, Mt. Nelson Hotel or Table Bay Hotel, Victoria Wharf and V&A Waterfront.

www.capetown.travel/

*FYI: If you buy a "hop on, hop off" bus pass, it includes stops at the major tourist attractions, which are too spread out to explore by foot. The pass is a good buy (one-day pass only or multi-day pass) and allows visitors to "hop on and hop off as they please.*

*Additionally, passengers are given headphones so they can enjoy an audio tour of Cape Town, which discusses the history and important facts about each place. However, both the Blue Bus and the Red Bus (two different routes) only go in one direction, so be prepared to ride the entire route or walk back to your destination.*

\*   \*   \*

**Table Mountain** overlooks Cape Town and is part of Table Mountain National Park. Its most noticeable feature is its level plateau that extends two miles and is flanked to the east by Devil's Peak and to the west by Lion's Head (more about Table Mountain later in this chapter).

**Kirstenbosch National Botanical Garden** is situated at the base of Table Mountain. This 1,300-acre garden dates back to 1913 and since that time it has only cultivated indigenous plants. It is the most famous national botanical garden in South Africa and also contains a conservatory.

**V & A Waterfront** is home to **Table Bay Hotel, Victoria Wharf Shopping Centre, Amphitheatre, Cape Grace Hotel, Cape Town Diamond Museum and Two Oceans Aquarium.** As the name implies, the aquarium has aquatic displays from

both the Indian and Atlantic Oceans,
including penguins and sharks.

**Castle of Good Hope** is the oldest
edifice in South Africa. This castle
fortress, built in the late 1600s, is now
a museum and popular tourist
attraction.

**Iziko Slave Lodge** was once slave
quarters for those working in the
Company's Garden. Today,
Company's Garden is a large public
park that includes botanical gardens.
Don't be surprised if squirrels come
stand on their hind legs in front of you
to ask for a treat. I have seen them
jump in the laps of those who have
food to share. Seriously!

**Grand Parade** was once a fort, later
a parade and exercise area for troops,
and is now a large flea market.

**City Hall** overlooks the Grand
Parade. It was built in 1905 and the
bell tower was added in 1923. The
Italian Renaissance structure actually
faces four different streets.

**South African Jewish Museum**
offers interactive exhibits chronicling
the history of Jews in South Africa.

**South African Museum and
Planetarium** has a bit of everything
pertaining to natural history, from
rock art to reptile fossils.

**South African National Gallery**
features temporary and permanent
collections of British, French, Dutch,
Flemish, and South African paintings,
sculptures, textiles, photography,
beadwork, and more.

**District Six Museum** serves to
commemorate the former District Six
are of Cape Town. At one time, it was
home to more than ten percent of the
city's population. The museum was

established in 1994 when apartheid finally ended. It has an incredible collection of street signs, photographs, documents, and recordings.

**Long Street** is one of the main streets of the city and can be easily recognized even without a map as the street is lined with exquisite Victorian buildings, which include intricate wrought-iron balconies and other special features. At one time, it was the longest street in the city.

**St. George's Mall** can also be easily recognized as it is home to many street performers and has a huge pedestrian area in its center.

**Adderley Street** is also easy to identify as it is the flower market, so visitors can see and smell gorgeous flowers of every imaginable kind. It is considered the main street of Cape Town.

**Greenmarket Square** is a large open-air craft market where African curios, leather goods, clothes, paintings, and more can be purchased.

**House of Parliament** is the official seat of the South African government. This building dates back to 1884.

Many different religions are practiced in Cape Town, so lots of different religious structures can be found, such as **The Mosque in Longmarket Street**, **Lutheran Church** on Strand Street, and **St. George's Cathedral**, which is an Anglican cathedral with beautiful stained glass. **Groote Kerk** is South Africa's oldest church. Only the steeple remains from the original church, which was rebuilt circa 1840.

*Blue Crane is National Bird of South Africa*

\*    \*    \*

**More Things to do in Cape Town**

**Milnerton Flea Market**. Everything from books and paintings can be found here every Saturday and Sunday. FREE.

Visit the Planetarium **at Cape Town Astronomical Observatory**. A night tour is offered on the second Saturday of each month. FREE.

The **Book Lounge** is considered the best independent bookshop in all of South Africa, so it is well worth a visit. Located in an old Victorian building in Roeland Street, visitors will find every kind of book including bestsellers, coffee table books, and rare books.

**Robben Island** is seven miles from Cape Town in the middle of Table Bay. Three hour tours include a visit to the 400-year-old prison, which was also a leper colony at one time. The most famous resident of this prison was Nelson Mandela. He was incarcerated here for most of his prison term. There are several other sites on the island, including a lighthouse and Governor's House.

For the über adventurous: take an **underground**

**tour of Cape Town** that extends from Buitkenkant Street all the way to the Castle of Good Hope.

For more Cape Town visitor information, www.capetown.travel/

\*   \*   \*

### *Warning:*

*Make sure that Table Mountain is open before setting out. The mountain often closes due to high winds, even if it isn't windy in town. Conditions change fast and fog often appears, blanketing the mountain and earning it the nickname 'Table Cloth.' The cable car does not operate in bad weather.*

*There are a hundred different paths to the top of Table Mountain, but the most popular ones are clearly denoted. It takes an average of three hours to ascend to the top. You can even do both, if you like. You can take the cable car up the mountain and then meander down the mountain on foot or hike up to the top and take the cable car down.*

*If it is a nice day, be sure to do Table Mountain even if you had planned to see other sights as the weather is unpredictable in Cape Town. There are posted signs that will let you know if the mountain is closed.*

## More You Should Know About Table Mountain...

Table Mountain National Park runs north-south along mountain range of Cape Peninsula. The park is separated by urban areas so it is actually made up of three different areas:

     1. Table Mountain (including Signal Hill, Lion's Head, and Table Mountain)
     2. Silvermind-Tokai
     3. Cape Point (Cape Peninsula)

www.sanparks.org/parks/table_mountain/

\*    \*    \*

There is an old legend about a Dutchman named Jan van Hunks, who got into a smoking contest with a stranger while up at Devil's Peak. The competition went on for days before the stranger admitted defeat and confessed his identity. He introduced himself as the Devil just before scooping up the Dutchman and disappearing into a cloud of smoke. Bellowing puffs of smoke lingered there long after they were gone. According to legend, when Devil's Peak is blanketed in clouds, it is believed to be the Devil coming back.

*　　*　　*

**Cape Peninsula Tour**...One of my favorite experiences is driving Chapman's Peak Drive up the coastline to Cape Point. During this twenty-five mile scenic drive, you'll pass Millionaires Paradise (a stretch of coast filled with expensive homes from Clifton to Camps Bay). This is literally a breath-taking view as there are no guard rails along the cliffs! During this drive, you'll see Green Point and Sea Point, Hout Bay, Noordhoek, Simon's Town (including

Boulder's Beach and African Penguins), Fish Hoek Beach, and Muizenberg. Be sure to stop and take a seal island cruise. There is wildlife at the Point, such as ostriches, Cape Mountain Zebras, and baboons.

At Cape Point, you can pose with signs denoting the "South-western most tip of Africa," which cites the exact latitude and longitude. Visitors can also take the cable car or hike up to the abandoned lighthouse, where there is a nice gift shop and good viewing. Visitors need to know that the baboons can be dangerous if you try to get too close for a photo opp. They can also be a threat to your belongings as they are notorious for climbing into vehicles and running away with camera bags, purses, and other items. I have heard a few stories about tourists losing their wallets and passports to thieving baboons.

There are lots of memorable experiences here so be sure to allocate enough time at Cape Point.

**Five Things You Should Do:**

1. Ride the funicular up to the top (or it is an easy-to-moderate hike) where there is an old lighthouse and great view of the cape. The cable car is called *Flying Dutchman*, so named after a legendary ghost ship.
2. Dine outside and enjoy the view and food at Two Oceans Restaurant.
3. Shop for great (and cheap) souvenirs and gifts at the shop, at the top of the cliff. But even if there is bad weather or you don't want to walk or ride the cable car to the top, there are

two shops at the base of the mountain.

4. Pose for a picture in front of the Latitude and Longitude sign for Cape of Good Hope.

5. Look for flora and fauna, wildlife and shipwrecks. There are 250 bird species here, as well as ostriches, baboons, elands (largest mammal in world), and Cape Mountain Zebra. You'll also find more than 1,000 indigenous plants that don't grow anywhere else in the world. If you take shipwreck trail, you will have a chance to view a few of the 26 recorded shipwrecks around Cape Point.

\*  \*  \*

*FYI: The southernmost tip of Africa is not Cape of Good Hope! It lies 155 kilometers southeast of Cape Point at* **Cape Agulhas***. When this was realized, the government barely acknowledged this distinction except to change the sign at Cape of Good Hope to read*

*"The Most South-Western Point of The African Continent."*

\*    \*    \*

*FYI: There are several good places in South Africa to see sharks but Cape Town area (Gansbaai) is among the best. About 160km from Cape Town lies Dyer Island, which is home to the largest seal colony in South Africa. Great*

*White Sharks can be found wherever there is food, such as seals. There are at least a half dozen companies that offer shark cage diving at 'Shark Alley'.*

*You can contact the SA tourism office for a complete list but a couple of companies I recommend are Shark & Safari Tours & Shuttles, www.sharkandsafari.co.za, and Apex Shark Expeditions, www.apexpredators.com.*

If you'd like to see a shark without having to go cage-diving, the best bet is at False Bay (Muizenburg), where there are shark spotters on duty. They have assigned positions along the beach like lifeguards. Watch for flags on the beach, which mean that sharks have been spotted that day. If you hear a siren, that means a shark has just been spotted SO GET OUT OF THE WATER!

About Great White Sharks…

Did you know that a Great White Shark can weigh over 7,000 pounds and be as long as 26 feet? I guess that's why it is the world's largest predatory fish!

Whale-watching is another popular pastime. Peak whale-watching season is from mid-August to mid-November but it really depends on the species as to the best time as there are thirty-seven species of dolphins and whales that can be found in the waters around South Africa. You can take a whale watching cruise. One good company that offers this option is New Fusion (www.newfusion.co.za) or can catch a glimpse from certain vantage points along Chapman's Peak Drive. Land sightings are most common at Hermanus and False Bay. Southern right and humpback whales have been seen as close as a mere ten yards from shore!

The male reaches maturity at around 13 years old and the female at 20 years old. The average litter is 7 – 9 pups. The females reproduce only twice in their lives. Their diet consists of all other marine life! They like seals, dolphins, and all fish. They are powerful enough to be able to propel themselves all the way out of the water. They have pointed snouts and razor-sharp teeth.

\*    \*    \*

**Dining in Cape Town...**

There are so many great places to shop, eat, and drink in Cape Town that a comprehensive list is impossible. However, I have noted some exceptional possibilities here:

**BEST PLACE TO HAVE A BEER:** Brewers & Union and Power & the Glory offers craft beer, delicious hot dogs and great music.

**BEST PLACE TO HAVE A BEER IF YOU'RE A HIPSTER:** Superette, Skinny Legs, and Clarkes

**BEST PLACE TO HAVE A COCKTAIL:** Societi, Bistro's Snug Bar, and Rafikis

**BEST PLACE FOR PIZZA**: Beluga and DaVincis

**BEST PLACE FOR PASTA**: Cocoa Uda

**BEST PLACE FOR AMBIENCE**: Ritz and Greenhouse (The Cellars-Hohenorrt Hotel)

**BEST BRUNCH**: Skinny Legs

**BEST PLACE FOR SALADS AND SANDWICHES**: The Kitchen

**BEST PLACE TO HAVE A BURGER:** Dog's Bollocks

**BEST PLACE FOR MEXICAN:** El Burro has the best food and serves tequila.

*FYI: The best places to shop are at Victoria & Albert Waterfront, Green Market Square, Long Street, the area around the Two Oceans Aquarium (and the aquarium has a souvenir shop), and Kalk Bay. The best place for nightlife is at Dockside, a gigantic temple-shaped building that houses fashionable bars, restaurants, and a huge ultra-hip discotheque that can hold up to 5,000 people.*

**BEST PLACE FOR COFFEE & TEA**: Deluxe Coffeeworks, EspressoLab and Origin (in the back is Nigiro, a must for tea drinkers) and Lady Cupcake (for tea and best cupcakes)

**BEST PLACE FOR ICE CREAM:** Roxy's and Mr Pickwicks

**BEST PLACE FOR CAPE MALAY FOOD** (Traditional Cape Town cuisine): Noon Gun Tea Room

*FYI: Cape Malay cuisine includes rice, coconut milk, and lots of spices!*

**BEST PLACE FOR NIGHTLIFE**: Waiting Room and Zula Bar

**BEST MARKETS**: Old Biscuit Mill, Neighbourgoods Market, and Bay Harbour Market.

*FYI: There is a large gay population in Cape Town. The visitor's center offers Pink Maps that highlight places of particular interest to gay visitors, such as an area of town known as De Waterkant.*

\*   \*   \*

 Spiritual Retreats

Where in the world could be better for spiritual rejuvenation than South Africa? Here are three retreats worth mentioning…

**Blue Butterfly Retreat** is located in the middle of Welbedacht Nature Reserve. It offers a mix of hiking, swimming, wildlife viewing, meditation, massage and yoga. http://www.thebluebutterfly.co.za/index.htm

**Hearth and Soul Eco Farm**, between Stanford and Napier is about as far away from it all as you can get. It doesn't even have a postal address! Participants can enjoy the solitude and partake in hiking, walking, yoga, meditation, and reading. There are 10 bedrooms with bathrooms, communal

dining areas, and a "hearth" room for socializing.
http://www.hearthandsoul.co.za/

**Satori Farm Eco Retreat** is situated high in the Natal Midlands, surrounded by mountains and water. Participants can choose from reiki, Pilates, yoga, workshops, massage, and meditation, as well as communing with nature.
http://www.satorifarm.co.za/

\*   \*   \*

## Western Cape

In addition to massive mountain ranges, there are valleys of fertile winelands. Many believe that no visit to South Africa is complete without a trip through the Cape Winelands. There are plenty of places to visit given that there are five dozen wineries in Stellenbosch, two dozen wineries in Franschhoek, and seventeen in Paarl. The Western Cape is also where Cape Town and Port Elizabeth are located.

When you hear the term **'Garden Route'** this refers to the coastline that meanders from Mossel Bay (just outside Cape Town) to

Grahamstown. Tourists appreciate the scenic 150-mile drive because the route is between the ocean and the mountains so plenty to see along the way. For example, Knysna Forest boasts more than 230 different species of birds.

Another popular spot on the Garden Route is Addo Elephant National Park, home to one of the largest elephant populations in South Africa. Port Elizabeth is a pretty port town that is popular with tourists. This route ends at Grahamstown, which has more than fifty churches and sixty national monuments.

www.gardenroute.org

# Highlights:

Cape Columbine Lighthouse, Knysna Forest, Cango Caves, Port Elizabeth, Addo Elephant National Park, West Coast National Park, Oudtshoorn (ostrich farms), and The Cape Winelands (most popular with tourists are Franschloek and Stellanbosch. Between Stellanbosch and Franschhoek is the Broschendal Manor House.

Other places in the Cape Winelands include Paarl, Worcester, Roberson, and Montagu). Most winelands tours will include a trip to the charming village of Franschloek and a trip over Helshoogte Mountain Pass to Stellenbosch. This is a scenic drive and a chance to see a part of Africa that looks quite different from safari country, as well as wine-tasting and sightseeing in these quaint towns.

www.wineland.co.za/

**Cape Columbine Lighthouse**, commissioned on October 1, 1936, is the last manned beacon in South Africa. It also holds the distinction of being the first lighthouse to receive three navigational aids: a fog signal, radio beacon, and light.

**Knysna Forest** is considered the 'pearl' of the Garden Route. Located between George and Plenttenberg Bay, it is known for its ancient yellowwood trees and stinkwood trees, which are home to many species of birds.

**Cango Caves** are near the town of Oudtshoorn, in the Western Cape Province of South Africa. Visitors are only permitted to go in supervised groups. There is a Standard Tour (1 hour) and an Adventure Tour (1.5 hour). The adventure tour includes some crawling through narrow passageways and climbing up steep rock formations guided only by small lights.

**Port Elizabeth** is the second largest city in this country, as far as size. Located on the Southeast coast of Africa, Port Elizabeth is a major seaport on Algoa Bay, which is the reason for its nickname "The Bay." It was established in 1820 to house British settlers. It is now part of the Nelson Mandela Bay Metropolitan Municipality, which has well over one million residents. It is best known for the many watersports it offers, as well as Shamwari Game Reserve, where the 'Big Five' can be found, as well as lots of other species of animals. www.portelizabeth.co/

**Addo Elephant National Park** is one of the biggest tourist attractions in this region and home to one of the largest elephant populations in South Africa; nearly 500. www.addoelephantpark.com

**West Coast National Park** is more than 100 square miles. It is considered an Important Bird Area (including African Oystercatchers and African Penguins) and home to large antelope, such as Mountain Zebra, Kudu, and Red Hartebeest, as well as Cape Gray Mongoose, Flamingos, and the Caracal. www.sanparks.org

*FYI: If you visit an ostrich farm at Oudtshoorn, be warned that ostriches eat just about anything and have been known to eat sunglasses, hats, and even buttons off their jackets or shirts.*

**Oudtshoorn** is the largest town in the Little Karoo region; home to approximately 60,000 residents. Its largest non-human population is the

ostrich since this is where most breeding farms in South Africa can be found. There are more than 400 ostrich farms here with the biggest being Highgate Ostrich Show Farm and Safari Show Farm.
www.outdtshoorn.info

**Cape Winelands** (includes several small towns as well as Franschloek, Paarl, and Stellanbosch). The climate and soil of the Western Cape make this region one of the best wine producing places in the world. It is ideal for growing Sauvignon Blanc, Chardonnay, Cabernet Sauvignon, Shiraz and Pinot Noir. A large number of the vineyards have restaurants on site. Some offer cheese tastings in addition to wine tastings. Typically, there is a small fee charged but may be refunded if wine is purchased or is included if taking a Cape Winelands tour. The Cape Winelands are easily accessible from Cape Town and can be explored

independently or on a tour. Most of
the vineyards are open during the
week and some on weekends.
www.wineland.co.za/

\*   \*   \*

**How To Speak Like A Local**...

I try to learn some phrases and common
words wherever I travel. Because there are
eleven official languages of South Africa, it
can be a challenge to try this. Here is a list
of common terms that will have you
speaking like a local:

**Bra** (Brah): A male who is a friend, buddy,
associate, peer, colleague, companion, travel
mate.
**China:** Slang used by surfers in Cape Town
and Durban areas to describe a
friend/buddy/mate.
**Chips**: warning meaning to "watch out!" or
"look out!"
**Chuck**: depart/leave/go.
**Crash**: Means to go sleep or crash.
**Dankie** (Dahn-key): Thank you.

**Dumela** (Doo-meh-lah): Greeting, as in "Good day."

**Hamba kahle**: Farewell/be well/ goodbye.

**Heikona**: Never! Not on your life!

**Hola** (Hh-O-lah): Greeting/hello.

**Howzit** (hoesit): "How's it going?"

**Isit** (Izzit?): Means "For real?"

**Just now/Now now** (nou- nou): If someone says he will do something "just now or now now" it could be in 10 minutes, tomorrow or he won't do it at all.

**Kaya** (Kai-yah): Hut or home.

**Lekker** (Leck-hah): tasty, nice, or fun. Ex: The food is lekker. (tasty) What a lekker! (fun)

**Ngiyabonga** (N-gee-yah-bong-ah): Thank you.

**Nooit** (Noy-t): No way!

**Padkos**: picnic

**Pull in:** Come in or to visit.

**Robot**: traffic light.

**Rock Up** To arrive. Ex: What time should we rock up?

**Sawubona** ('Sah-wu-bo-nah'): Greeting, as in "Good day."

**Skelm** (Skeh-lm): A crook or thief. Another common word for thief is Tostsi (Tsoh-tsee).

**Voetsek/Voertsek** ('Foot-sack'): Go away! Get lost!

\*   \*   \*

## Eastern Cape, Kwazulu-Natal and Free State

The **Eastern Cape** is punctuated by South Africa's highest mountains, **Drakensberg** (called the Ukhahlamba or "barrier of spears" by the Zulus), which run the length of this region. In addition to mountains, the Eastern Cape boasts beaches and picturesque resorts that extend for more than one hundred miles. **Durban**, the country's largest port, is situated in the northern part of the East Coast. To the north of Durban there is vast subtropical forests, lakes, and unspoiled savannahs filled with all kinds of bird species and wildlife.  This area,

**Kwazulu-Natal**, is also home to the Zulu, who are renowned warriors, dancers, and craftsmen. Tourists like to buy their beautiful baskets, pottery, mats, and beadwork. There is not much tourism in the **Free State**, even though it is situated in the heart of South Africa. The reason being that most of it is farmland. There are more than 30,000 farms in this province, which produces most of the country's grain. This explains why it is called South Africa's 'breadbasket'.

*FYI: Some of the world's best surfing can be achieved at Durban. Cave Rock is where the deep ocean channel and a reef create huge waves comparable to Hawaii's Pipeline. Mr Price Pro is South Africa's biggest surfing competition, a week-long even held every July since 1969. It was the first professional surfing contest held outside of Hawaii.*

## Highlights:

Golden Gate National Park, Durban and Zululand, and Wild Coast, Drakensberg and Midlands. Lesotho, known as "Kingdom of the Sky" encompasses Drakensberg (Dragon Mountains). This is a popular place for hikers, campers, and climbers. In Durban, visitors flock to the Golden Mile, a four-mile stretch of resorts, pubs, amusement parks, beaches, and restaurants. This area includes several game reserves, Croc World, and sharks. Up to fourteen different kinds of sharks swim the warm waters off Kwazulu-Natal. This includes the sand tiger, hammerhead, whale shark, Zambezi, and Great White. Sharks are so prevalent that shark nets have been constructed just past the surf –less than 550 yards from shore! More than 1,000 sharks are caught in these nets every year.

www.zulu.org/za/

**Golden Gate National Park** is in Free State, South Africa, near Lesotho. It is the only national park in this region. It stretches more than 130 miles and includes more than 100 bird species. It is famous for its colorful sandstone cliffs and caves featuring san rock paintings. www.sanparks.org

**Durban and Zululand**. The Zulu of KwaZulu and those in Natal Province merged, this garden province became known as KwaZulu-Natal. The capital is Pietermaritzburg and its largest city is Durban. It borders Swaziland, Lesotho, and Mozambique. This area is home to most of South Africa's sugar plantations. Durban is considered the Jersey Shore or Grand Strand of South Africa with its Golden Mile (which is actually four miles) of attractions, restaurants, and resorts. www.durban.gov/za/

*FYI: Five Fun Things To See & Do in Durban...*

*\*KwaZulu Sharks Boat Tour*
*\*KwaMuhle Museum*
*\*uShaka Marine World*
*\*Ianda Heritage Trail*
*\*Umhlanga Lagoon Nature Reserve*

**Wild Coast, Drakensberg and Midlands** can be found in the southern part of the East Coast and Interior. The Drakensberg Mountains are the highest mountains in southern Africa. The Midlands area landscape of green hills and forests, which house country hotels and dairy farms. The currents of the Indian Ocean have created the cliffs and coves of the

Wild Coast, which is best known for

The Hole in the Wall (commonly called the most romantic spot in South Africa).

This region is one of the least developed in South Africa but the perfect place for honeymooners, bird watchers, nature lovers, hikers, and fishermen.

**Lesotho**, also known as 'Kingdom in the Sky, has a unique relationship with South Africa because it is a landlocked country completely surrounded by South Africa. It is less than 12,000 square miles in size (and includes Drakensberg, Maluti, and Thaba-Putsoa Mountains) with a population of less than two million. The border between Lesotho and South Africa extends for 565 miles

and forms a complete loop.
www.wikitravel.org/en/Lesotho

**Free State** Province holds little
interest to tourists because it mostly
consists of large mineral deposits and
30,000+ farms.

\*   \*   \*

## Northern Cape

The Northern Cape includes all land <u>North of the Orange</u> [River] and <u>South of the Orange</u> [River]. While there are a few national parks, there is not much of interest to tourists South of the Orange. This area is mostly sheep farms. North of the Orange is the Kalahari Desert. This is for hardcore adventurers only as this is considered to be the last frontier. We're talking extreme temperatures (hot and cold), primitive lodging, Bakkie skiing (liability waivers required) and donkey cart rides! Just beyond this desert area lies Kimberly, which was where the world's great diamond rush took place. Digging of the "Big Hole" (Kimberley Mine) at Kimberley began in the 1870s. By 1873, more than 50,000 miners were here. By 1914, nearly 23 million tons of rock had been excavated from the Big Hole, yielding roughly 14 million carats of diamonds!

**Kalahari Desert** (Kalahari means waterless) is in the arid interior of South Africa and extends for more than 350,000 square miles across three countries: Botswana, Namibia, and South Africa. While there is little rainfall and high summer temperatures, the Kalahari does have significant plant and animal life, such as black-maned lions, brown hyena, wildebeest, and cheetah. In fact, the Central Kalahari Game Reserve is the world's second largest protected area. Only the Kalahari Bushmen knew this area until recently when the reserve opened to the public. There are a couple of camps here, but this pocket of South Africa is reserved for serious adventure travelers. **Kalahari Tours**

**& Travel** offers excursions into this area. http://www.kalahari-tours.co.za/

*FYI: Kimberley is the only stop on the Blue Train and includes a visit to the diamond museum and vault where a replica of the world's biggest diamond, Cullinan Diamond, can be seen. There is also a short, fascinating film about diamond mining. This is one of only four mines still in operation in Kimberley.*

**Kimberley** is the capital of Northern Cape Province, which lies beyond the Orange River. Its historical significance is due to its diamond mining past. The "Big Hole" is its biggest attraction, which is the world's largest hand dug excavation. It was created when thousands of people searched for diamonds during the late 19th and early 20th centuries.

Visitors enjoy seeing The Big Hole and Open Mine Museum. The museum is comprised of reconstructed and preserved buildings that showcase the town's history. The Eureka, the first recorded diamond discovered in South Africa, is on exhibit at this museum. There is a great film that documents the area's mining history.
www.kimberley.co.za/

\*   \*   \*

## Gauteng, Mpumalanga, North West and Limpopo

This is the heart and soul of South Africa, at least for safari enthusiasts. For here is where Kruger National Park and Pilanesberg Game Reserve can be found. In addition to Kruger, dozens of private game reserves are here and well worth a visit or stay.

Johannesburg is the largest city in South Africa. It has the highest population (roughly ten million) because it offers the most job prospects. Interestingly, it is not the capital city. Actually, South Africa has three capitals: Pretoria, Cape Town, and Bloemfontein. Johannesburg is the capital of the Gauteng Province, which is the smallest province in South Africa.

Limpopo has become a tourist destination for those wanting to venture off the beaten path. While this northernmost province is largely comprised of the Mapungubwe UNESCO World Heritage Site, it offers quite a bit more. This North West Province was created in 1994 when apartheid ended. It is west of Gauteng and is the northern gateway to Kruger National Park. But there's more than Kruger. Nature lovers will enjoy exceptional birding (including the rare raptor, Taita Falcon), hiking, and exploring the Waterberg Biosphere, Bela-Bela, Modjadi Cycad Reserve, and Blyde River Canyon Nature Reserve. There's also skydiving, jeep and horseback safaris, and golfing at Legend Golf and Safari Resort.

There are two private game reserves: Polokwane Game Reserve

and Welgevonden Game Reserve with four lodges: Ant's Nest Lodge, Kurisa Moya Nature Lodge, Mashovhela Lodge, and Shivuvari Lodge.

## Highlights:

Johannesburg (and Soweto), Sun City (Palace of the Lost City), Kruger National Park, Pilanesburg (Kruger's "cousin"), Gold Reef City (reconstruction of J'burg in 1890s), Pilgrim's Rest (a restored gold mining town from the 1800s), and Swaziland.

*Warning:*

*For those taking the Blue Train, you will depart from the city of Pretoria, which is not safe for independent exploration. Do not wander around on foot after dark and even in the daylight be careful of where you go. Crime is a huge problem in Pretoria and that is why most hotels and many homes are inside secure compounds.*

**Johannesburg** is the largest city in South Africa, at least population-wise. It is also the wealthiest province in the country. Johannesburg is also known as J'burg, eGoli, Jo'burg, Joeys, Jozi, and JHB. Interestingly, JHB is the world's largest city that is not located on a lake, river, or coast. JHB city tours include the Apartheid Museum, Gandhi Square, Constitution Hill, Carlton Centre, and Oriental Plaza. www.joburg.org.za/

**Soweto** is part of JHB, but was a separate city until the 1990s. Soweto (meaning **SouthWesternTo**wnships) is a collection settlements populated by residents who work in the gold-mining industry. It is best seen during a day tour and not recommended for independent exploration.

**Sun City**, including the legendary **Palace of the Lost City**, is 112 miles northwest of Johannesburg. This is a two or three-hour drive, depending on traffic and time of day. There are stretches of road that are one-lane so that can slow things down if it is rush hour or if there are a lot of trucks on the road. Also, it is a bit of a challenging drive in the dark as there are no streetlights and much rural area to cover. While Sun City has been described as Las Vegas meets Atlantis

(Bahamas), you will see that it is quite different and that this description does not do it justice.

As soon as you pull into The Palace, you'll see a magnificent cheetah sculpture fountain. After entering the inner courtyard, you'll be greeted by a huge elephant sculpture and atrium. Additionally, you'll be rewarded with a beautiful central fresco, exquisite and authentic safari furnishings, lagoon, twenty-five-acre botanical garden, and more.

Sun City is situated in the between Elands River and Pilanesberg National Park. While there are other places to stay in Sun City (The Cascades, The Cabanas and Sun City Hotel), I highly recommend spending the extra money to stay at the pinnacle of this place, The Palace of the Lost City. You will thoroughly enjoy all it has to offer, such as high tea and cocktails in its lovely lobby bar at night.

As a guest at The Palace you have access to all other areas of Sun City (but guests at other properties do not have access to The Palace. Everyone staying at Sun City has access to most of the casinos, fitness center, spa, waterworld, restaurants, shops, crocodile sanctuary, golf courses, Superbowl, and entertainment centre (cinema, restaurants, arcade, bar and shops). The Superbowl is their concert venue where many legendary singers have performed, such as Elton John, Rod Stewart, and Frank Sinatra. More outdoor options: quad bike rides, hiking, exploring, archery, clay pigeon shooting, horseback riding, http://www.sun-city-south-africa.com/ or www.suninternational.co.za

**Pilanesberg National Park** is considered the younger cousin to Kruger. It offers a more intimate safari experience. If staying for a few days at The Palace, I recommend going on a game drive or balloon safari at Pilanesberg. www.pilanesbergnationalpark.org

## Five Things You Should Do:

1. Elephant-back safari or a hot-air balloon safari over Pilanesberg
2. Night game drive in Pilanesberg
3. View of Sun City from King's Tower in The Palace at the Lost City
4. Behind-the-scenes orientation tour of The Palace at the Lost City
5. Play a slot machine in the public casino at Sun City. There are hundreds of machines that feature singers and celebrities, as well as classic TV and movie themes and

stars, such as Dolly Parton, Charlie's Angels, Back to the Future, and The Simpsons.

Pilanesberg National Park is a great experience for those wanting a more personal experience than Kruger. And like Kruger, there is no malaria risk. You can stay at Sun City and then head out early for the one hour drive to Pilanesberg or you can stay inside the park at one of the exceptional resorts. Pilanesberg Centre is in the center of the park and there are a half dozen lodges situated around the edges of the park. Bajubung Bush Lodge is the largest. Shepherd's Tree Game Lodge and Tshukudu Bush Lodge are the most luxurious while Buffalo Thorn Lodge

are self-catering facilities for the
budget-minded.
www.parksnorthwest.co.za/pilansberg

*FYI: Many movies and TV
shows are now being made in South Africa,
thanks to its diverse topography and
incentives. It has been dubbed the "New
Tinseltown."*

**Kruger National Park** is one of the
largest game reserves in Africa. You
shouldn't go to South Africa without
visiting Kruger, which is on South
Africa's northeast border and runs
along the border of Mozambique to
the east, Zimbabwe to the north, and
Crocodile River in the south.

More than one million visitors
a year pay pilgrimage to this
enormous wildlife sanctuary, which is

the same size as New Jersey (USA) and is the same size as the entire country of Israel.

It is divided into fourteen different eco-zones and is home to many species of wildlife, as well as flora and fauna. Its largest water source is the Olifants River.

This flagship of the South African Parks System was established in 1898 by South African President Paul Kruger. It was twenty-nine years later before its gates opened to the general public. All of the "Big Five" can be found in Kruger and surrounding game reserves: Cape Buffalo, Leopard, Lion, Elephant and Rhino. The "Big Nine" include those mammals plus Hippo, Giraffe, Cheetah, and Zebra.
www.krugerpark.com

*Did you know…*you can see Baobab trees in the north part of this park, as well as 379 other indigenous trees?

*Did you know…*there are 16 different sections to this park?

*Did you know…*there are 507 bird species, 116 reptile species, and 34 amphibian species here?

*Did you know*…there are more than 5,000 giraffes here?

*Did you know*…more than 3,000 hippos make their home here, as well as 146 other mammal species?

*Did you know*…the park is most populated with Impalas (150,000) and the least populated with cheetahs (200)?

*Did you know*…all camps have elevated viewing platforms for optimal wildlife viewing?

**Since Kruger is so big, where's the best place to visit in this park?**

That depends on what you want...

**Northern Kruger** is the most remote.
Lots of elephants, buffalos, and
antelopes can be found here. There
are several lodging options: Punda
Maria (huts), Mopani (camp),
Shingwedzi (camp) and Letaba
(chalets). Note: Letaba is the most
upscale of the Northern Kruger
lodging options. Or you can stay in
Limpopo and drive into Northern
Kruger, thus having two different
safari experiences.

**Central Kruger** features impalas,
zebras, wildebeest, giraffes, buffalos,
lions, and elephants. There are two
camps: Olifants and Satara.

**Southern Kruger** is only about one-
fifth of the park but gets fourth-fifths
of the park's visitors. This is because
it offers the best wildlife viewing with

the most species and all of the Big Five. Three of the five biggest camps in Kruger are here: Sabi Sand Game Reserve, Manyeleti Game Reserve, and Timbavati Game Reserve (Gomo Gomo Game Lodge). Additionally, there is Klaserie, which includes several private reserves. A great place for a walking safari is at Plains Camp in Southern Kruger. www.sanparks.org/parks/kruger

 For more information on any of these places, www.sanparks.org.

For a map detailing all the reserves and parks in the Gauteng province, http://www.sa-venues.com/accommodation/ga_game_lodges.htm.

For a complete list of health

resorts and spas in Gauteng province,
http://www.sa-
venues.com/hotels/healthspas-
gauteng.php

\* \* \*

**All About Safaris…**

*Where should I stay while on safari?*

You can **stay in a private game reserve** with a lovely lodge and all the amenities. Typically, airport transfers, meals, and guided game drives are included in the package. Game drives take place in the early morning and afternoon/evening. Most packages include two game drives per day. Most lodges have indoor and outdoor dining areas, a spa, a pool and lounging deck, a bar, a small gift shop, and comfortable communal areas.

Something to consider when making your plans is that within the national park vehicles must stay on the roads. In these private game reserves, vehicles can (and often do) go off road. This is important because most animals do not stay on the roads. Prices vary according to the lodge and its amenities (and seasonal specials and promotions). $$-$$$$$.

Another option is to **stay in a rest camp**. These are the opposite of game lodges. All national parks, including Kruger, offer this option. Participants camp in a tent, caravan (camper), or whatever lodging is offered, such as wooden huts, cabins, or chalets. Public restrooms are available and meals can be bought on site or campers can prepare their own braai using the camp's grills and picnic areas. Some prefer this rustic experience as it feels more authentic to a safari experience. You should be aware that when choosing this option you have made the choice to participate in a self-guided safari unless you pre-arrange to have a guide. Rest camps are popular because they are so affordable, even to South Africans who earn low wages, so be sure to book EARLY.

Another option is to **stay in both places**! Stay a few nights in a rest camp and then move into a four-star lodge—enjoy the best of both worlds.

When staying in a lodge at a private game reserve, you have more safari options. You can go on a **group safari drive** whereby you share a jeep with a group (other guests staying in the same lodge at the same time); **hire a private guide**; or **rent a vehicle and go on your own**.

*FYI: You may hear about other options, such as hostels, guest houses and cottages but these are elsewhere in South Africa—not in the parks or reserves.*

I do not recommend this last option for several reasons. One reason is that you sometimes have to go off-road to pursue the most elusive mammals, such as the cheetah and leopard. You can get stuck, which has happened on every safari I've been on. This is no big deal when you have a guide as he calls another driver in the area and they quickly pull the jeep out in no time at all. Or you could get lost or have car trouble. More importantly, when you have a guide you will see more animals as they are in communication with other guides and also know where to go and when to see certain animals. Besides, it is a more enjoyable experience to sit back and watch and listen rather than having to navigate dirt roads and figure out where to go next. The guides also share good stories and useful information.

*FYI: Safari is a Swahili word, which means 'journey'. You will journey into a new place unlike any you've ever seen before; full of wonderful wildlife and amazing scenery—and some of the friendliest people in the world.*

## Safari terms...

"braai" is a big outdoor barbecue held at safari camps

"biltong" is dried meat

"boerewors: traditional sausage served at "braai" along with chicken, steak, chicken, snoek, lamb, kebabs, crayfish, and game meat

"boma" is the open thatched entertainment center used for communal gatherings at safari camps

"Koeksister" is a traditional Africa dessert. It is a sweet cake made of yeast dough that is deep-fried and dipped in syrup

Some tourists choose to make a quick visit to **Swaziland** while in this area.

It is the smallest country in Africa.

It is the last absolute monarchy in Africa.

Swaziland is well known for its culture. Special events include Umhlanga, held in the month of August/September, and Incwala, the dance of the kingship held in December/January.

Highlights: Milwane Wildlife
Sanctuary, Mbabane, Peak Craft
Center, Hlane Royal National Park
and Malolotja Nature Reserve.
www.welcometoswaziland.com

\*   \*   \*

Here is a list of the major parks and reserves throughout South Africa including safari options:

- **Addo Elephant National Park** is one of the best parks for classic safaris; Big 5 but rarely see elephants here.
- **|Ai-|Ais Richtersveld Transfrontier Park** is more about hiking and scenery than safari; no Big 5.
- **Dhuma GR** is a large private reserve at Sabi Sand that offers Classic safaris; Big 5.
- **Exeter Leadwood GR** is a large private reserve at Sabi Sand that offers Classic safaris; Big 5.
  **Golden Gate Highlands NP** has few animals but great hiking and scenery.
- **Hluhluwe-Imfolozi GR** is a a big game resere that offers Classic safaris; Big 5 especially rhinos.

- **Idube GR** is an exceptional private reserve at Sabi Sand; Big 5.
- **Inyati GR** is a large reserve at Sabi Sand that offers Classic safaris; Big 5.
- **Kapama Private GR** has four different lodges throughout Greater Kruger offering Classic safaris; Karoo National **ParkKgalagadi TP** offers Classic safaris in Botswana; good population of big cats.
- **Kruger National Park** offers Classic safaris; Big 5.
- **Lion Sands GR** is a private reserve at Sabi Sand that offers Classic safaris; Big 5.
- **Londolozi GR** is a large reserve at Sabi Sand that offers Classic safaris; Big 5.
- **Madikwe Game Reserve** is one of the largest reserves that offers Classic safaris; Big 5.
- **Mala Mala GR** is a big reserve in Greater Kruger that offers Classics; lots of wildlife including Big 5.
- **Mkhuze Game Reserve** offers Classic safaris; Big 5.

- **Phinda Game Reserve** offers Classic safaris; lots of wildlife including Big 5.
- **Pilanesberg Game Reserve** offers Classic safari; Big 5.
- **Sabi Sabi GR** offers Classic safaris at various private reserves throughout Greater Kruger; Big 5.
- **Shamwari Game Reserve** large reserve offers Classic safaris; Big 5.
- **Singita GR** at Sabi Sand offers Classic safaris; Big 5.
- **Tembe Elephant Park** is a large park that offers Classic safaris; Big 5 (especially elephants)
- **Timbavati NR** offers Classic safaris in Greater Kruger; Big 5 and rare white lion.
- **Waterberg Biosphere Reserve Area** contains many game reserves Marakele NP.

Animal Sightings...

In addition to the "Big Five," you can
see all kinds of other wonderful
animals (according to region). You
can either create a safari animal
checklist or use one of these handy
apps while on safari:

**African-Safari Wildlife Guide** can be
downloaded before leaving home so that no
Internet connection is needed. iPhone &
iPad. $.
https://itunes.apple.com/us/app/id341885050
?mt=8

**The Kingdon Guide to African Mammals**
includes close to 500 species. iPhone, iPod
touch & iPad. $.
https://itunes.apple.com/us/app/id336901877
?mt=8

**Audubon African Wildlife** includes mammals, birds and reptiles. iPhone & iPad. $.
https://itunes.apple.com/us/app/id378562356?mt=8

**Africa: Live app** is my favorite. It offers real-time safari sightings with live maps and interactive markers, plus live social media streams and the ability to add sightings and upload photos. Android and Apple Smartphones. FREE.
https://itunes.apple.com/us/app/id552879842?mt=8

**Wildlife of Southern Africa** is another app I love because it has info and images for trees, spiders, insects, frogs, reptiles, birds, and mammals. It offers more than 2,500 species throughout Southern Africa. Blackberry, Android, and Apple. $.
https://itunes.apple.com/us/app/id333269795?mt=8

Guides are well-trained to know all the animals so they will quickly identify any and all animals you spot while on safari. However, if there is a bird or reptile they don't recognize, they have wildlife encyclopedias and

will quickly find the answer for you.
What you won't see on any
safari is the Quagga. The animal's
front end resembles a zebra but it
looks like a horse in the rear. It has
been extinct since the late 1800s.

The Quagga (above) is not to be
confused with the Cape Mountain
Zebra, which is elusive but not extinct

*   *   *

## Best Beaches in South Africa

For beach lovers and water sports enthusiasts, no visit to South Africa is complete without a visit to at least one of its many beaches. Some of these beaches have been rated the best in the world (blue flag beaches). In addition to all the normal activities, including swimming, walking, sunbathing, and picnicking, other activities can be achieved at certain beaches as denoted.

**Eastern Cape**

Hobie Beach (surfing + sailing), Port
Elizabeth

Humewood Beach, Port Elizabeth

Kings Beach (surfing), Port Elizabeth

Nahoon Beach, East London

Gonubie Beach, East London

iSimangaliso Wetland Park (whale
watching) Cape Vidal

Umhlanga Rocks (surfing + boogie
boarding) Durban

Dolphin Coast, KZN

Margate and Ramsgate (popular with the
locals) KZN

Sodwana Bay (fishing + beach driving)

South Beach (surfing) Durban

*These Durban beaches offer lots of
nightlife and eclectic cafes and shops.

North Beach (surfing) Durban

## Western Cape

*There are close to seven dozen beaches in this region offering a wide variety of 'sun and fun' activities.*

Camps Bay is arguably the best beach in the Western Cape. Camps Bay.

Clifton is actually four beaches and a favorite of celebrities and locals.

Boulders Beach (penguin watching) is part of Table Mountain National Park, Simon's Town.

Hermanus is a small village with a lot to offer tourists besides Grotto Beach including the Old Harbour Museum, shark cage diving, Whale Festival (annual spring migration of Southern Right Whales), and the best whale watching in South Africa. Something that is really cool (and a great photo opp) is the Hermanus Whale Crier. He blows his kelp horn to announce sightings. It is something to see—and hear!

Muizenberg (family beach), Muizenberg

Noetzie (there are three castles on the beach), Knysna

Lookout Beach, Plettenberg Bay

Robberg Beach (whale watching), Plettenberg Bay

Buffels Bay, beside Plettenberg

Bikini Beach, Gordon's Bay

Strand Beach, Strand

Mnandi (fishing) Mitchells Plain

Strandfontein (biggest tidal pool in Southern Hemishphere) Mitchells Plain

Fish Hoek (surfing +kitesurfing) Fish Hoek

Long Beach (surfing + windsurfing) Kommetjie

Hout Bay

Milnerton Beach (windsurfing) Milnerton

Llandudno

Big Bay (surfing + kitesurfing + windsurfing) Big Bay

Sandy Bay (nudists like this beach), next to Llandudno

Silwerstroom Strand (fishing + boat launch)

*FYI: The beaches can be quite hot from October – March in South Africa. Expect them to be very busy and charge peak prices during the Christmas holiday. Despite the heat, the waters of southern South Africa remain cold year round. The water is colder on the Atlantic Ocean side (Western Cape) than it is on the Indian Ocean side (Eastern Cape).*

\*     \*     \*

Important Information:

**VAT:** When shopping for souvenirs and gifts, be sure to get receipts. You have to pay Value Added Tax (VAT) on most goods, which is fourteen percent. You should get a refund document from the store (you won't get such a document from a street vendor), especially if buying jewelry, art, antiques, clothing, collectibles, home furnishings and such. If you do much shopping, this can add up so be sure to keep track of your purchases.

You can only get VAT back at the airport, so allow time BEFORE YOU CHECK IN FOR YOUR FLIGHT to go to the VAT office and show your documents. Sometimes they will ask to see the items you're claiming so be prepared that you might have to open your luggage, which is why I emphasized doing this before you check your luggage. Unfortunately, the VAT people do not issue money.

They give you a form that you have to take to a money exchange booth where they will ask if you'd like South African currency or some other currency. Your inclination will be to get currency of your country since you are headed home. However, I highly recommend South African currency because the conversion fees and exchange rate is ridiculous. You only get pennies on the dollar when all's said and done. But if you get local money, the rate and fee is not bad.

You can shop at the Duty Free airport shops after you check in for your flight and check your luggage. Be sure to check in for your flight before you go shopping. You don't want your seat given away or your luggage being refused because you lost track of time. Besides, you don't want to have to keep an eye on your luggage or drag it around with you while shopping. There are lots of great shops at Johannesburg airport where you almost assuredly will be flying out of, but there are shops at the Cape Town and Durban airports too. Here you can buy everything from toiletries to African art. Or you might opt to spend the money on a nice meal and cold drink at one of the many dining outlets before your long flight.

**TIPPING:** South Africans depend on tips. Their wages are low and they work hard to please visitors. You'll see! Suggested amounts will be provided to you by management and probably posted in your room or on your travel documents from your tour operator. As a general rule, you should tip ten to twenty percent of your bill. On safari, your guide and tracker should each get $5 - 10 per day. Typically, guests put $5 - $10 a day in an envelope and give it to management, who dispenses it accordingly. If you have a staff member who has gone the extra mile, feel free to give him more money.

**Blokart Sailing**

**SPECIAL INTEREST VACATIONS:** There are so many activities available—just about everything you can imagine—and then more! Adventurers can choose from blokart sailing, hiking, rambling, kloofing, rock climbing, fishing, hang gliding, paragliding, bungee jumping, sky diving, canopy tours, zip lining, cycling, river rafting, pony trekking, horseback riding, bird watching, golfing, diving, shark cage diving, whale watching, rail travel, safaris, and other tours, such as cultural tours, nature/photography tours, wine tours, ghost tours, and battlefield tours.

## RAIL TRAVEL:

If you want to use the train to get somewhere or just want to include a train ride because you like rail travel, you have some choices.

**Shongololo Express** (most casual and basic of trains). Nice but not exceptional. No toilets or showers in cabins. $$. www.shongololo.com

**Rovos Rail.** This is a deluxe, vintage train that carries only 72 passengers in all-suites with private bathrooms. It is all-inclusive including off-train excursions. $$$$. www.rovos.co.za

**Blue Train**. Think Orient Express. All the suites have televisions with lots of free movie options. The food and service is exceptional. It is all-inclusive, even cocktails and afternoon tea, plus an excursion to the famous Kimberly Diamond Mine Here you'll see the "Big Hole" and diamond museum. $$$$$. www.bluetrain.co.za

*FYI: The trains have limited schedules, so which train you choose may come down to what's running where you're going when you're going to be there.*

\*    \*    \*

*What To Pack...*

*raincoat and jacket or heavy coat
(depending on season)

*sturdy walking shoes and good socks

*clothes that can be layered as it can
be cold in the mornings and evenings
and hot during the day.

*hat/visor/cap

*gloves and scarf (depending on
season)

*sunscreen

*insect repellent

*bathing suit and cover up

*shower shoes/sandals (for bathing, swimming, and spa visits).

*nice outfit, such as long, black skirt and dressy blouse with suitable shoes

*casual clothes (pants, shorts, t-shirts)

*undergarments

*sleeping attire

*alarm clock

*watch (don't pack jewelry except cheap costume jewelry)

*toiletries, comb/hairbrush, glasses/contact lenses/sunglasses

*book or tablet/reader (optional)

*cell phone (optional)

*travel documents

*cash/credit cards/travelers cheques

*chargers and extra batteries for iPod, phones, cameras, etc.

If you're planning on doing any special interest activities, be sure to pack what you need for that, such as a prescription mask if going snorkeling or shark diving. All companies provide wetsuits and masks but not prescription masks.

*hiking shoes and good socks

*prescription medications

*over the counter meds (such as aspirin, seasickness pills, antacids, bandages, and topical ointment, such as Neosporin®)

Be sure to pack the right clothes. If it is winter (remember their seasons are opposite) when you visit, be sure to pack pants and a coat and scarf. If it is summer there when you visit, be sure to pack lightweight, comfortable clothes.

*converters and adaptors if you have an electric razor, curling iron, mobile phone/tablet, hair dryer (most hotels and lodges have hair dryers but self-catering camps will not) or if you think you'll need to charge your camera batteries or will have some type of medical equipment that requires an outlet.

Note: 220/230 V; Plug M. I recommend investing in a universal adapter and converter kit. You'll have what you need wherever you go. You must have a converter as well as an adapter.

Keep in mind when packing…

Clothing is quite casual during safari
but there is a dress code on Rovos
Rail and the Blue Train. During the
day it is smart casual but in the
evenings formal wear is required.

This means jackets
for men and elegant attire for women.
However, the train personnel are not
too strict about the dress code. Men
can get away with wearing a jacket
without a tie and women can wear a
fancy top with a nice pair of pants or
skirt. Any shoes but sneakers will be
fine. They understand that you are on
safari (most likely) and so you have
weight restrictions on your luggage.

*FYI: Be sure to check for the latest updates from TSA so that you know what you can and can't take on the plane in your carry-on bag or pack in your suitcase. Also, you should check with your airline regarding their latest baggage restrictions (and baggage fees). There is a weight limit and acceptable sizes for both carry-on bags and checked luggage, which varies according to the airline. Certain items are banned or restricted to three ounces or less and limited to certain types of containers, as determined by TSA.*

*These restrictions are subject to change periodically. <u>http://www.tsa.gov/traveler-information/packing-tip</u>*

\*   \*   \*

**TRAVEL DOCUMENTS**: Be sure to keep a copy of your itinerary and emergency contact information with you at all times. Keep copies of every ticket and confirmation to show if needed. You must have a valid passport to enter South Africa. If you're an American or European citizen that is all you will need unless you are staying for more than ninety days. If you're from certain European cities (Cyprus, Hungary, Poland and Slovak Republic), you can only stay for thirty days without a visa. If you're going to Swaziland, you need a Visa but you can get one at no charge at the border. If you're going to Lesotho, there are some visa restrictions depending on your nationality. For more on passports and visas, http://www.passportsandvisas.com/

Give a copy of your itinerary including contact information to a relative or close friend. You may also want to consider checking in with your embassy. The government has a free service called STEP or Smart Traveler Enrollment Program. U.S. citizens and nationals traveling abroad can sign up prior to leaving the States. The benefits include:

Receive important information from the Embassy about safety conditions in your destination country, helping you make informed decisions about your travel plans. Help the U.S. Embassy contact you in an emergency, whether natural disaster, civil unrest, or family

emergency. Help family and friends get in touch with you in an emergency.
https://step.state.gov/step/

**TRAVEL INSURANCE**: Anytime you travel outside of the U.S. (especially adventure trips), I recommend travel insurance. Do a little research or ask your travel agent for recommendations. www.Travelexinsurance.com and www.travelinsured.com are two good options.

**TRAVEL WARNINGS:** At the time of publication, the only travel warning for South Africa was for travel to Lesotho. However, things can change so it is best to go to http://travel.state.gov for latest news. Also, be sure to check on the latest regarding visas, passports, and required (and recommended) inoculations.

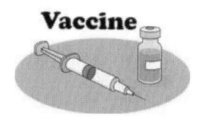

**VACCINATIONS:** None are necessary but some parts of South Africa are prone to malaria. Anti-malaria medication is not required but should be obtained if you are traveling to such an area.
Additionally, you may need a yellow fever certificate (this comes from your local county health department) to travel to certain areas. Check for health concerns for areas you may be flying in or out of, as well.
http://www.vaccines.gov/travel/ and http://wwwnc.cdc.gov/travel

**FOOD & WATER**: The government says that tap water is safe in most of South Africa as it is chlorinated. However, I always err on the side of caution and drink bottled water when I travel. Food is just something you have to use common sense about consuming. You want to try new things, after all that is the point of travel. But at the same time, you might not be excited about pigeon pie or monkey brains. If something looks or smells or tastes disagreeable, don't eat it. I always travel with protein bars in case I get hungry between meals or in lieu of a meal. I hate airplane food and pigeon pie!

\* \* \*

*FYI: Here are some authentic South African dishes you may want to try while in country:*

### Bunnychow

Hollow out a loaf of bread and pile it high with a mountain of lamb curry, and you have the deliciousness known as bunnychow. Fillings are not limited to curry either: the many "bunny" purveyors around the country often get creative with the contents. Bunny chow is served in newspaper and eaten with your hands, and can be ordered in quarter, half, and full loaf sizes. It's most common around Durban, but can be found throughout South Africa.

### Biltong

If you like beef jerky, you'll love biltong. It's dried, cured meat produced in long, thick strips and flavored with various spices. It can be made from beef, fish, chicken, or

game animals like springbok and
ostrich.

## Bobotie

Bobotie (boo-BOO-tee) is kind of like
shepherd's-pie-meets-moussaka, with
curried mincemeat, onions and an
egg-custard topping. It's baked like a
casserole and served with bay leaves
and chutney. This dish originates with
the Cape Malay people, who are of
mixed Indian-Indonesian heritage. It
is considered the national dish of
South Africa.

## Koeksisters

Koeksisters (cook-sisters) are a sweet
doughnut-like treat. They're made of
pastry dough which is deep-fried and
then dipped in a syrup.

## Boerewors

Although they don't look all that
appealing, (boor-eh-voors) is a tasty

sausage made from ground beef or pork mixed with South African spices. It originated on rural South African farms, hence the name (boerewors literally means "farmer sausage"). Typically formed into a big spiral, "boeries" are great food for a braai (barbecue).

**Chakalaka**
This super-spicy spicy vegetable relish originated in the townships of South Africa and has been a staple for generations. Made of tomatoes, onions, peppers and beans, it's usually served over pap (maize meal), with slices of bread or as a condiment for grilled meat.

**Melktert**
Melktert literally means "milk tart." It's similar to a British custard tart, but lighter and fluffier. After being baked, the tart is sprinkled with cinnamon. Melkterts date back to the arrival of the Dutch in the 17th century, and the recipe hasn't changed

much since then. They are a great
accompaniment to afternoon tea.

## Braai

As mentioned earlier, Braai means
South African barbeque.

\*     \*     \*

**THE PEOPLE**: It goes without saying—yet I am saying it because it is such an important point—travelers should always be respectful of other cultures. Not only are you a guest in their country, but you are also an ambassador to your homeland. Your behavior reflects on all people of your native country. Not only should your behavior be exemplary, but you should also dress appropriately.

**SAFETY**: As with any travel, you are putting yourself out there. Despite any attempts you make, it will probably be obvious that you are a tourist so be sure to exercise common sense. Look around. Pay attention. Don't wander off down a dark, side street alone. If

you're out and about and notice that
you have entered a desolate or seedy-
looking area, hightail it back to a
congested area. Don't count your
money on the street corner. Don't
wear expensive jewelry. Don't call
attention to yourself. Don't carry
much money on you each day. Don't
put your wallet in your back pocket or
carry a purse. Be careful to safeguard
your passport and other travel
documents.

**ATTITUDE**: Traveling can be so
rewarding and fun. But at times it can
be challenging, like when a flight is
delayed or cancelled. Or when you
have some kind of bad experience,
like the air conditioning not working
in your room or getting Montezuma's
Revenge. If you come prepared,
you'll be all right.

If you have done your
homework so that you know what to

expect and you bring the right stuff (documents, money, meds, etc), that's half of it right there. The other half is attitude. You have to be flexible and adaptable when traveling to the other side of the world.

Think of all the great stories you can tell when you get home. Sometimes, what seems like a bad situation can lead to something good. I've met some of the greatest people and had some of the best experiences as a result of a detour or delay.

**HEALTH**: If you have a health condition, such as heart trouble or diabetes, you should consult your doctor before taking any trip. You also need to check with the authorities to find out if you need a letter from your doctor (if taking injections or narcotics) and there are airline rules about carrying oxygen and some types of inhalers.

Be sure you talk to your doctor before getting any vaccinations to make sure they won't interfere with any meds you're on. I have heard of people suffering from mild hallucinations while on anti-malaria medication and certain motion sickness drugs. I have taken both and never had any adverse reactions but you should discuss this with your doctor and pharmacist, who probably knows more about side effects than your doctor.

**MONEY**: Make sure you have enough in the

right denomination. I recommend the 1/3 system, which is 1/3 cash in small bills and 1/3 credit card (two different ones) and 1/3 travelers cheques. You don't have to do this, it's just a recommendation based on my experience. You may get somewhere that doesn't take credit cards. It happens more than you think in foreign countries, especially developing countries. Travelers cheques are in case your wallet or bag gets stolen, you can replace those on the spot.

You need to authorize your credit card company to approve overseas transactions as most will block them now due to credit card/identity theft. Even then, you may find they have 'frozen activity' on your account. That's why I recommend a back-up credit card. Check the transaction fees and rates (and balances and rewards) before deciding which card to take.

You can even opt for a pre-paid

travel credit card. Both Visa and MasterCard are widely accepted, but Discover and American Express are not as widely accepted.

You can exchange cash at exchange bureaus at the airport or at a bank or even your hotel. Make sure you do that before you leave for a less populated or remote destination on your trip. While on safari, most lodges will accept South African Rand or you may charge to your room. They don't take foreign currency or travelers cheques. They will, however, accept credit cards.

Keep your contact information separate from your travelers cheques and credit cards. If they get stolen, you will have the information you need to replace the travelers cheques and cancel the credit cards. You don't want to wait until you get home to do that as it will be too late by that time.

*   *   *

## *VICTORIA FALLS...*

*Many people mistakenly believe that Victoria Falls is in South Africa. In actuality, this waterfall is in southern Africa but not in South Africa. The falls are on the Zambezi River at the border of Zambia and Zimbabwe. Many trips will offer an optional three-day extension to see Victoria Falls.*

*You can drive to the falls if you have time but another option is a flight from Johannesburg to Livingstone on South African Airways. Great places to stay if you Exceptional lodging options include the David Livingstone Safari Lodge and Spa (www.thedavidlivinstone.com) and Victoria Falls Safari Suites (http://www.africaalbidatourism.com/safari-lodges/victoria-falls-safari-suites).*

*While there, you may want to*

*partake in one of these optional activities:*
*sundowner cruise on the Zambezi, helicopter*
*ride (known as helicopter flips!), hiking, or*
*you can do a fun and easy Zimbabwean walk*
*(entrance fee to this area), bungee jumping*
*off the bridge, elephant-back safaris,*
*swimming in Devil's Pool, sunset steam*
*train ride to see the falls, and whitewater*
*rafting on the Zambezi.*

*Be sure to bring a raincoat and*
*protective bagging for your camera because*
*of the spray from the falls. The rainy season*
*is from mid-November to mid-April.*

*The falls are in a malaria area so*
*you need to be on anti-malaria medication*
*and you will need a yellow fever certificate*
*to enter Zambia. Additionally, you will need*
*a Visa if you do not have a SADC passport.*
*Be sure to get a multi-entry Visa if staying*
*for a few days to avoid paying for a permit*
*every time you cross the border.*

*Be sure to have enough cash (small*
*bills) with you for your stay as most vendors*
*do not accept credit cards and ATMs are*
*scarce. For tourism information pertaining*
*to Victoria Falls,*
http://www.zambiatourism.com/destinations
/waterfalls/victoria-falls

## Sample 14-Day Itinerary

This itinerary can be altered to suit your interests, timeline, and budget. Build onto this sample itinerary if you are able to stay longer than two weeks. I don't recommend going to South Africa is you have less than two weeks. I just don't think this is enough time. It is a long journey and there is so much to see and do that you need at least two weeks so that you won't feel cheated or short-changed. I have seen week-long packages offered (and you may be tempted by the price) but I wouldn't recommend these trips.

Instead, scale back on optional activities if you're looking to save money. Remember that you can stay in economical rest camps rather than pricier lodges while on safari. There are so many wonderful things to see and do in South Africa (and so many ways to experience them) that you can't go wrong unless you don't stay long enough or don't do sufficient planning.

Day #1: Arrive a.m. in Johannesburg. Go to **Palace of the Lost City**; optional activities (See Palace discussion for a list of activities). Depending on availability, the Palace usually offers a complimentary room upgrade upon check in. Nice!

Day #2: **Pilanesberg Game Reserve** (hot-air balloon safari and/or game drive) and dinner and drinks at Palace.

**Day #3: Sun City**; optional activities (orientation tour of The Palace only offered once a day). Eat dinner at one of the other hotel restaurants and check out the casino. Even if you don't gamble, you should see the slot machines and maybe play just one.

**Day #4:** Morning at leisure. Drive back to Johannesburg and short flight to Hoedspruit Airport to start safari with **night game drive** at your private game reserve.

**Day #5: Safaris at Game Reserve**

Note: There are optional activities you can enjoy in between your two daily game drives, such as a **visit to a nearby village, spa treatment, cheetah conservation center tour, and elephant interaction**. Or you can sunbathe, swim, read, nap, talk to fellow travelers, and write postcards. You can even arrange an extra safari for an extra fee. All meals are included: early a.m. coffee, juice, and

snack before first game drive,
breakfast (after first game drive),
lunch, afternoon tea/refreshments
(before evening game drive), and
dinner (after evening game drive).
Cocktails are usually not included.

Day #6: **Safari at Game Reserve**

Day #7: **Safari at Kruger National
Park**

Day #8: morning **game drive** and
then fly to J'burg and overnight at
hotel in nearby **Pretoria**. Have a nice
dinner and go to bed early.

Day #9: 7 a.m. depart from Pretoria
on **Blue Train** (overnight). This
includes stop at Kimberly. All meals
and beverages (including cocktails)
included, as well as afternoon tea.

Day #10: **Blue Train** arrives at mid-day at **Cape Town**. After checking into hotel, take free shuttle to V & A Waterfront and do some shopping and enjoy a nice meal.

Day #11: **Cape Town sightseeing** (hop on, hop off bus) & **Table Mountain**. See Cape Town discussion for list of sightseeing options.

Day #12: **Cape Peninsula Tour**

Day #13: Cape Town (**shark cage diving or other optional activities**)

Day #14: **Wild Card Day**. Last chance to do anything in Cape Town, such as Table Mountain (if weather hasn't been suitable), afternoon tea at Table Bay Hotel or Nelson Hotel, and nightlife on Long Street or Cape Winelands Tour or Garden Route Tour, which is Cape Town to Port Elizabeth.

\*　　\*　　\*

*FYI: You can schedule a stopover on route home. Depending on your route, you could spend a day or two in Cairo, Egypt; London, England; Frankfurt, Germany; or Paris, France. There are many routes to South Africa that you may want to consider this while you are still in the planning stages. You can alter your itinerary to have one less day on safari or in Cape Town and still keep to a two-week vacation. The same holds true if there is something else you'd like to see or do, such as Victoria Falls or Swaziland.*

\*　　\*　　\*

**Resources**

There are many good resources and references that discuss South Africa's history and culture. Here are a few recommendations:

**South African Tourism** is the official tourism site, http://www.southafrica.net/landing/visitor-home

**Department of Tourism** is another government resource: http://www.tourism.gov.za/

**Tourism** in **South Africa** (Wikipedia) http://en.wikipedia.org/wiki/Tourism_in_South_Africa

**South Africa Travel** offers unofficial tourist information, http://www.southafrica.com/

**Cape Town Tourism** is the official website for Cape Town, http://www.capetown.travel/

**Southern Africa Tourism Services Association,** http://www.satsa.co.za

**South Africa National Park** is the official site for all SA park information, www.sanparks.org

**South Africa Tour Operators** provides a list of all companies that operate in SA, http://www.safaribookings.com/operators/south-africa or you can obtain a list of reputable companies that offer South Africa packages from the U.S. Tour Operator Association. http://www.ustoa.com/

**Thompsons Holidays** is my favorite resource for SA tours. They are a Cape Town company that is used by many top tour operators, http://www.thompsons.co.za/travel/aboutus.cfm

For a list of **travel agents** specializing in South Africa trips, check out the American Society of Travel Agents, http://www.asta.org/

For a list of **hostels** throughout South Africa, www.hostelworld.com

**National Parks & Game Reserves in South Africa** (A-Z List). http://www.safaribookings.com/parks/south-africa

**South Africa Accommodations** (from hotels to hostels to five-star lodges) (http://staynow.com/destinations/south-africa/safari-lodge.aspx and http://www.sa-venues.com/south-africa-lists.htm

## **Kruger National Park** | South African Safari and Lodging Guide
http://www.krugerpark.co.za/

Other good resources include the **Bed and Breakfast Association of South Africa** (www.babasa.coza) and **Guest House Association of Southern Africa** (www.ghasa.co.za) and South Africa Hostels (http://www.hostels.com/south-africa), www.SouthAfrica.net and www.SouthAfrica.info

\*     \*     \*

Here is a list of good publications:

<u>MAPS</u>

**South Africa: National Geographic Adventure Map**

**South Africa Map** (Globetrotter)

**Kruger National Park Map**
(Globetrotter) L.E.O. Braack

**South Africa Game Reserves Map**
http://www.nature-reserve.co.za/south-africa-nature-reserves-map.html

## REFERENCES

*South Africa* (Insight Guides). For more on SA art, music, wine, and flora and fauna.

*DK Eyewitness Travel: South Africa* (good maps, photos, and general history)

*Culture Smart! The Essential Guide to the Customs & Culture of South Africa* (Kuperard Publishing) David Holt-Biddle. Discusses the culture and beliefs of the people, as well as offers insights and etiquette advice.

*The Safari Companion: A Guide To Watching African Mammals* (Chelsea Green Publishing) Richard P. Estes

\*   \*   \*

## Special Dates & Events

The following is a list of public holidays:

**New Year's Day** (January 1)

**Human Rights Day** (March 21)

**Good Friday** (April)

**Family Day** (April)

**Freedom Day** (April 27)

**Workers' Day** (June 16)

**National Women's' Day** (August 9)

**Heritage Day** (September 24)

**Day of Reconciliation** (December 16)

**Christmas Day** (December 25)

**Day of Goodwill** (December 26)

\*  \*  \*

This is a list of major annual events throughout South Africa:

**Cape Town International Jazz Festival** (April)

**Fire-Walking** (April)
This is an annual event for devout Hindus. Believers who have prepared spiritually will test their faith by walking across red-hot coals (without pain or injury).

**National Arts Festival** (July)

**Mr Price Pro** (July) Big Surfing Competition

**Whale Festival** (September) Every year in late September lots of whales and their calves can be seen when they come unusually close to shore.

**Carols by Candlelight** (December)

**Miss South Africa** (December)

**Nedbank Golf Challenge** (December)

**FNB Dance Umbrella** (February)

**Summer Sunset Concerts** (January) Outdoor musical concerts that take place all over Cape Town area

\* \* \*

**South Africa Quiz**

1. The African Penguin was once called:
   a. Gentoo Penguin
   b. Emperor Penguin
   c. Jackass Penguin
   d. Tuxedo Penguin

2. Johannesburg was established after what was found there?
   a. Diamonds
   b. Gold
   c. Oil
   d. Salt reserves

3. How many official languages are there in South Africa?
   a. 1
   b. 2
   c. 8
   d. 11

4. What is the highest mountain range in South Africa?
   a. Everest
   b. Himalayas
   c. Drakensberg
   d. Dranesburk

5. The west coast of South Africa is home to the largest mainland colony of what?
   a. Lemurs
   b. Flamingos
   c. Seals
   d. Penguins

6. Nelson Mandela is important to South Africa history because of his role in what?
   a. Zulu War
   b. Apartheid
   c. Diamond mining
   d. Boer War

7. What was the first game reserve in South Africa?
   a. Sabi Sands
   b. Lost City
   c. Kruger
   d. Pilanesburg

8. What product has increased in exports post-apartheid?
   a. Diamonds
   b. Wine
   c. Sugar
   d. Gold

9. What city in South Africa has been voted the best place in the world?
   a. Johannesburg
   b. Pretoria
   c. Cape Town
   d. Durban

10. How many capital cities does South Africa have?
    a. 1
    b. 2
    c. 3
    d. 6

\*   \*   \*

## South Africa Quiz Answers

1. c
2. b
3. d
4. c
5. c
6. b
7. c
8. b
9. c
10. c

TERRANCE ZEPKE

*A Picture Is Worth*

*A Thousand Words...*

**Aaahhhhhhhhhh!**

**Break time in the bush...nice!**

**Cape Buffalo is one of the "Big Five."**

**My, what big teeth you have!**

**I was so happy to get this photo as it's an
unusual site to see a giraffe lying down.
They only do it when sleeping and we just
happened to catch this guy waking up!**

**Double trouble!**

**See how close you get to the animals…and
sometimes even closer!**

**Zebras are one of my favorite animals but they're also among the most skittish so get your photo quickly.**

**Safari participants will see lots of small animals too, such as this cute Meerkat.**

**Upon landing at the small airport, safari guides are waiting to whisk travelers off to respective camps to begin their adventures!**

**Kapama Game Lodge is on Kapama
Game Reserve, one of the private reserves
in Greater Kruger.**

**Game lodge interior…not bad, huh?**

**One optional activity is hot air ballooning.**

TERRANCE ZEPKE

**Cape of Good Hope**

**Robben Island is where Nelson Mandela
spent part of his 27-year prison term.**

**Shark cage diving is as close as you'll ever want to be to a Great White Shark!**

There are spectacular sculptures and carvings throughout Sun City, which is the largest resort hotel complex in the world.

**African Penguins (also known as Jackass Penguins) are abundant at Boulders Beach.**

 **Oudtshoorn is home to more than four hundred ostrich farms.**

**Dead end!**

**Simon's Town is at False Bay, on the
eastern side of the Cape Peninsula. it is an
important naval base and harbor for the
South African Navy, as well as a popular
tourist spot.**

The tower of the Cape Town City Hall
has a marble façade and turret clock with
a face that's made from skeleton iron
dials filled with opal. The building was
constructed from limestone imported
from England. It houses the library and
concert hall.

**This Cape Town photo includes the V &
A Waterfront with Table Mountain in the
background.**

**The oldest and most colorful area of Cape
Town is Bo-Kaap. It reminds me of
Rainbow Row in Charleston, SC.**

**Blue Train Bar Car**

## The food is delicious aboard the Blue Train.

**Rovos Rail Dining Car**

TERRANCE ZEPKE

**Durban Coastline**

**The Zulu are the largest ethnic group in
South Africa with the biggest population
residing in KwaZulu-Natal.**

## Titles by Terrance Zepke

### Travel Guidebooks:

*The Encyclopedia of Cheap Travel: Save Up to 90% on Lodging, Flight, Tours, Cruises and More!* (Lookout Publishing)

*Terrance Talks Travel: A Pocket Guide to South Africa* (Safari Publishing)

*Terrance Talks Travel: A Pocket Guide to African Safaris* (Safari Publishing)

*Terrance Talks Travel: A Pocket Guide to Adventure Travel* (Safari Publishing)

*Coastal South Carolina: Welcome to the Lowcountry* (Pineapple Press)

*Lighthouses of the Carolinas* (Pineapple Press)

*Spookiest Lighthouses: Discover America's Most Haunted Lighthouses* (Safari Publishing)

*Spookiest Battlefields* (Safari Publishing)

*Coastal North Carolina* (Pineapple Press)

*A Ghost Hunter's Guide to The Most Haunted Hotels & Inns in America* (Safari Publishing)

*A Ghost Hunter's Guide to The Most Haunted Houses in America* (Safari Publishing)

*A Ghost Hunter's Guide to The Most Haunted Places in America* (Safari Publishing)

## Ghost Books:

*The Best Ghost Tales of South Carolina* (Pineapple Press)

*Ghosts of the Carolina Coasts* (Pineapple Press)

*Ghosts and Legends of the Carolina Coasts* (Pineapple Press)

*The Best Ghost Tales of North Carolina* (Pineapple Press)

*Ghosts of Savannah* (Pineapple Press)

## Special Interest Titles:

*Happy Halloween! Hundreds of Perfect Party Recipes, Delightful Decorating Ideas & Awesome Activities* (Safari Publishing)

*Lowcountry Voodoo: Tales, Spells and Boo Hags* (Pineapple Press)

*Pirates of the Carolinas* (Pineapple Press)

**Books for Kids** (8 – 12 years old)

*Ghosts of the Carolinas for Kids*
(Pineapple Press)

*Pirates of the Carolinas for Kids*
(Pineapple Press)

*Lighthouses of the Carolinas for Kids*
(Pineapple Press)

\*     \*     \*

**For more information on these books and for FREE TRAVEL REPORTS:**
www.terrancetalkstravel.com **and** www.terrancezepke.com

**Listen to her travel show on**
www.blogtalkradio.com/terrancetalkstravel

**You can follow @TerranceZepke on Twitter to receive #terrancetalkstravel tips**

**Or you can connect with her on Facebook, Google+ and Pinterest**

\*     \*     \*

Notes

TERRANCE ZEPKE

# Index

# TERRANCE TALKS TRAVEL: A POCKET GUIDE TO SOUTH AFRICA

Safari Publishing

37603882R00128

Made in the USA
Charleston, SC
12 January 2015